THE UNCOMMON SINGLE JOURNAL

Writing Prompts, Quotes, and Inspirations

Nicole Porter

authorHOUSE®

AuthorHouse™
1663 Liberty Drive
Bloomington, IN 47403
www.authorhouse.com
Phone: 1 (800) 839-8640

Published by AuthorHouse 12/04/2017

ISBN: 978-1-5462-1948-4 (sc)
ISBN: 978-1-5462-1949-1 (hc)
ISBN: 978-1-5462-1947-7 (e)

Print information available on the last page.

This book is printed on acid-free paper.

Book Testimonials for *The Uncommon Single*

"This was definitely a book of motivation and self discovery. This awesome writer took us on a journey through hurt and growth to let us all know we are not alone in our own struggles and after the storm and tests we all will have a testimony to rejoice in. I look forward to reading future books from this wonderful author."

April Ward, Medical Transcriptionist/Case Specialist

The Uncommon Single came into my life at pivotal time as I transitioned from being married to being single. It reassured me that I can handle this new season in my life and not only go through it, but also grow through it! This book rocks!!!

Carlene C. Wright, CEO of Wright Encouragement and the Host of the Wright Encouragement Show

"Very inspirational!!! Best book I've read all year! Single, married and dating women all can benefit from this amazing guide to a healthy and happy relationship."

Terry-Ann Porter, CEO of Simply Royal Events

"The Uncommon Single is a quick, but quality read. Ms. Porter's transparency and thought provoking questions allowed me to feel her frustration, pain, and ultimate triumph. I loved the use of scripture reference because it is important for readers to realize that there is a Sovereign Being that wants to guide our lives, if we allow Him. Also, "The sweet benefits of being single" found on page 25, should be framed and hung on every women's wall. Overall, this book has valuable information that will be life changing, readers will not be disappointed."

Kerry-Ann Connell, Writer and Editor

"Excellent book, she was very open and honest and that's what people need in these days. I commend her for sharing her story to let others know that there is life after a divorce/breakup, you cannot depend on a man/woman to make you happy. Please get your copy TODAY!!!!!!"

Diane Porter, Accounts Payable Specialist

"This book is worth every penny! I was amazed at the authenticity, transparency, and passion she wrote with but also how she was able to overcome all she endured. As a man, I too was able to identify and relate to a lot of the hurt and disappointment she went through but also the processes and measures to take on the road to recovery and in being refined and fortified. The insight that was shared can and will certainly help anybody who is currently or that has gone through a relationship breakup. This book has helped me even now. I would definitely recommend this book as a Must Have! Big ups!!!"

Pernell Durran Gurice, Actor, Entrepreneur

"The Uncommon Single is a honest, to the point guide on how to be an uncommon Single. The book is an easy read with great points that can relate to many people single or married."

Shaneka Walstine, Educator

"Powerful book and testimonies. My favorites were the letter dedication to her future husband and prayers for my future husband. This was powerful, as a now married woman, these are conversations that I've had with God concerning my now husband. I believe when we ask, it shall be given unto us. Words have power and when we write the vision and make it plain, His word shall not return to us void. This was the best quick read and very understandable. As a married woman, I continue to grow in Christ and can learn from this book. I will keep this on my shelf, as a constant reminder of the miracles of God. I believe that God has great things in store for you and your future husband."

Stephanie Sicar, CEO of WifeStyle of Faith

"Very insightful, transparent, and practical. I loved how she used her pain as a stepping stone for her personal, spiritual and mental growth, and then took all that she learned and was willing to share with others and encourage those who may be experiencing the same pain. A beautiful testament of the fact that "we are not what we go through.""

Keesha Barreau, Makeup Artist, Entrepreneur

"As a guy I thought the book would be more of a woman's guide to liberalism or something of the like. But as I read it I found it to be helpful and educational to both male and female alike. And a very quick and powerful read as well. I have a young teenage daughter who is dealing with relationship problems of her own and I bought another book just so I can give it to her. Great job Nicole, keep up the good work."

Owen Clark, Fort Lauderdale, Florida

"I absolutely Adore Nicole, she has done something that most people wouldn't dare do. She has allowed God to use her mess and transform it to a Message... The Bible says that we overcome by the word of our Testimony! In this book, Nicole shares her testimony! She exposed her wounds from an area in Marriage that the "church folks" don't want to talk about. Her story will encourage singles to seek God first for their future spouse and not give in to their feelings and that future mate checklist. Additionally, there's a 14-Day prayer guide for them to pray for a future mate. May God bless her and those that read this book!"

Avi Ambroise
Research &Training Specialist

PRESENTED TO:

_____

BY

_____

OCCASION

_____

Table of Contents

Introduction

This Journal is the companion guide to *The Uncommon Single, Turning Mistakes into Stepping Stones for Success.* It is highly recommended that you read the book prior to leveraging this journal.

Journaling facilitates personal growth. It is effective whether you are just writing whatever comes to mind or whether you are journaling on a specific topic.

It helps to clear the mental clutter and improve overall focus. It's impossible not to grow because whether it's about achieving goals or becoming a better person, or whatever you use it for, you'll eventually see yourself growing as a person.

HOW TO USE THIS BOOK

The Uncommon Single journal is divided into four sections based on my book, *The Uncommon Single.* It's an open door to self-discovery, so step through and begin the amazing journey toward living an uncommon life.

This book is meant to be written in. Write yourself little notes of encouragement and fresh ideas that come to you. In this journal, you'll find thought provoking questions, encouraging scriptures and simple prayers to help you focus your heart and mind on living an uncommon life to the fullest. Take some time to reflect and ponder the questions. Allow the scriptures to speak to you.

Whether or not you've ever journaled before, *The Uncommon Single* Journal will inspire you to write openly and freely about your daily experiences.

STEP ONE:

DEALING WITH DISAPPOINTMENTS

Principle 1

No Bitterness Over Brokenness

As you continue to grow, raise your standard for love

TRANSFORMING TRUTH:

A bitter root will produce a bitter fruit. If you want to elevate your life, you must be quick to forgive. Learn to let go of the hurts and pains of the past. Don't let bitterness take root in your life.

PONDER THIS: Dare to check the root of your fruit. If you're harboring anger, ask yourself why. When you get to the root, you'll be able to deal with the problem, overcome it, and can truly begin to change. I encourage you to refuse to be bitter over brokenness! Let God's love restore you.

Begin to accept today as a fresh new opportunity. Let each passing day stay in the past. Let today be your day of unfolding hope, faith, and love.

Writing Prompt

This cannot be happening…

_____

_____

_____

_____

_____

_____

_____

_____

_____

_____

_____

_____

_____

_____

_____

_____

Writing Prompt

I feel insecure when…

_____

_____

_____

_____

_____

_____

_____

_____

_____

_____

_____

_____

_____

_____

_____

Writing Prompt

I am not sure I can do this anymore…

_____

_____

_____

_____

_____

_____

_____

_____

_____

_____

_____

_____

_____

_____

_____

_____

Inspiration:

In the space below, List all the things that you are grateful for and why.

_____

_____

_____

_____

_____

_____

_____

_____

_____

_____

_____

_____

_____

_____

_____

_____

WHAT THE SCRIPTURES SAY:

He heals the brokenhearted and binds up their wounds.

Psalm 147:3

Looking carefully lest anyone fall short of the grace of God; lest any root of bitterness springing up cause trouble, and by this many become defiled;

Hebrews 12:15

A PRAYER FOR TODAY:

Heavenly Father, I thank you that all things are working together for my good and that my best days are still ahead.

_____

_____

_____

_____

_____

_____

_____

TAKEAWAY TRUTH: Forgiveness is the key to being free. Today, do your best to reject thoughts of limitations and failure in your mind and replace them with empowering words of truth, victory, joy, peace, and happiness.

Principle 2

Find Strength Through Adversity

*The next time you walk into love, make it
a decision to love intelligently.*

TRANSFORMING TRUTH:

God often is working the most when we see and feel it the least.

PONDER THIS: Adversity often pushes us into our divine destiny. One of the best ways to reach the next level of your life is to use adversity to your advantage.

Writing Prompt

What challenges have you overcome?

_____

_____

_____

_____

_____

_____

_____

_____

_____

_____

_____

_____

_____

_____

_____

Writing Prompt

What life lessons have adversity taught you?

_____

_____

_____

_____

_____

_____

_____

_____

_____

_____

_____

_____

_____

_____

_____

_____

Writing Prompt

In what ways have you been allowing adversity to impact your joy?
Your passion? Your life?

_____

_____

_____

_____

_____

_____

_____

_____

_____

_____

_____

_____

_____

_____

_____

_____

Inspiration:

In the following space, record all the reasons you're proud of yourself. List as many things you can think of, big or small.

_____

_____

_____

_____

_____

_____

_____

_____

_____

_____

_____

_____

_____

_____

_____

_____

WHAT THE SCRIPTURES SAY:

We are hard pressed on every side, yet not crushed; we are perplexed, but not in despair; persecuted, but not forsaken; struck down, not destroyed.

2 Corinthians 4:8-9

Many are the afflictions of the righteous, but the LORD delivers him out of them all.

Psalm 34:19

A PRAYER FOR TODAY:

Heavenly Father, I'm determined not to let adversity defeat me. You are the source of my strength and very present help in my time of trouble. Father, I ask for your wisdom to navigate this season of my life.

_____

_____

_____

_____

_____

_____

_____

_____

TAKEAWAY TRUTH:

No matter what adverse events whether big or small, you are currently experiencing, there is always a purpose behind each one. After you have experienced an adverse event, you will be at a crossroad. You can either view it as a blessing or allow your past to dictate the rest of your life.

Principle 3

Out with The Old, In with The New You

Become a better woman and you will attract a better man.

TRANSFORMING TRUTH:

When gardeners prune bushes, they cut off dead or ugly branches. They do this for two reasons: to improve the appearance and to produce growth.

God does the same thing with us. You know the baggage and guilt we all carry around? He helps us rid our dead branches, those things that have become apart of us through life's trials. Sometimes we are reluctant to let go of it, but it is this baggage, these dead and unsightly branches, that keeps us from flourishing in God's grace. If we allow God to prune away these dead branches, we will be more ready and able to grow in our faith, as beautiful individuals designed in God's image, for His purpose.

PONDER THIS: Envision the future that you'd like to have one day. What God has for you is bigger than your past. God is always ready to do new things in our lives. The question is, Are you ready? Are you making room for it in your own thinking?

Writing Prompt

I have no more patience for…

_____

_____

_____

_____

_____

_____

_____

_____

_____

_____

_____

_____

_____

_____

_____

Writing Prompt

When will it be my turn...

_____

_____

_____

_____

_____

_____

_____

_____

_____

_____

_____

_____

_____

_____

_____

Writing Prompt

I failed today because…

_____

_____

_____

_____

_____

_____

_____

_____

_____

_____

_____

_____

_____

_____

_____

Inspiration:

In the space below, write about a time when you were proud of yourself for turning a negative situation into a positive one.

_____

_____

_____

_____

_____

_____

_____

_____

_____

_____

_____

_____

_____

_____

WHAT THE SCRIPTURES SAY:

Behold, I will do a new thing, now it shall spring forth; shall you not know it?

Isaiah 43:19

He has put a new song in my mouth. Praise to our God; many will see it and fear, and will trust in the LORD.

Psalm 40:3

A PRAYER FOR TODAY:

Heavenly Father, You're my keeper. Thank you for crowning me with glory and honor.

_____

_____

_____

_____

_____

_____

_____

_____

_____

_____

TAKEAWAY TRUTH:

Development is happiness. I think that we invest in ourselves according to our self-image. I encourage you to take the time to learn and heal from your previous relationships.

STEP TWO:

PROGRESS IS
A PROCESS

Principle 4

Dare to Be Extraordinary

The way you see yourself sets the standard for how others treat you.

TRANSFORMING TRUTH:

You will never rise above the image you have of yourself in your own mind.

Preparation time is never wasted time. God doesn't reveal everything to us instantly. He puts us through a *process.* It requires an ongoing trust, obedience, steadfastness, and faithfulness.

Many women daydream of that special day. The gorgeous white dress, the flowers, the decorations, the limousine and let's not forget, the Prince Charming. A lot of us want things that we are not prepared for.

PONDER THIS: Singleness highlights your individuality and uniqueness. I want to encourage you to truly surrender to God in this season and just rest knowing that the best is still yet to come.

Writing Prompt

Are you prepared for what you're praying for?

_____

_____

_____

_____

_____

_____

_____

_____

_____

_____

_____

_____

_____

_____

_____

_____

_____

Writing Prompt

What are some things that would make your future brighter?

_____

_____

_____

_____

_____

_____

_____

_____

_____

_____

_____

_____

_____

_____

_____

_____

Writing Prompt

Life is not fair because…

_____

_____

_____

_____

_____

_____

_____

_____

_____

_____

_____

_____

_____

_____

_____

_____

WHAT THE SCRIPTURES SAY "But those who wait on the Lord shall renew their strength; they shall mount up with wings like eagles, they shall run and not get weary, they shall walk and not faint."

Isaiah 40:31

For as he thinks in his heart, so is he.

Proverbs 23:7

A PRAYER FOR TODAY:

Heavenly Father, I thank you for another day and for brand new mercies. Help me to become a better person today than I was yesterday.

_____

_____

_____

_____

_____

_____

_____

_____

_____

_____

_____

Inspiration:

In the space below, write about the future you envision for yourself?

_____

_____

_____

_____

_____

_____

_____

_____

_____

_____

_____

_____

_____

_____

_____

TAKEAWAY TRUTH:

What we believe about ourselves have a much greater impact on our lives than what anybody else believes. Become what you believe. Start seeing yourself through eyes of faith.

Principle 5

Your World Is a Mirror

*The type of man you choose is a direct
reflection of how you see yourself.*

TRANSFORMING TRUTH:

Everything that you are is mirrored back to you. It is simply the reflection
of your own state of consciousness. Faith is defined as having confidence
or trust in something or someone. Sometimes it's hard to stay faithful
when everything in the natural seems so hopeless. We should make a
decision to be determined to walk by faith and not by sight.

PONDER THIS: Speaking the promises of God over your life is
one thing, but are your actions lining up to what you are professing?
Whatever it is you want to be, become it by studying successful people
and emulating what they do.

Writing Prompt

I am not over the fact that...

_____

_____

_____

_____

_____

_____

_____

_____

_____

_____

_____

_____

_____

_____

_____

_____

_____

Writing Prompt

Sometimes I feel…

_____

_____

_____

_____

_____

_____

_____

_____

_____

_____

_____

_____

_____

_____

_____

_____

_____

Writing Prompt

I am disappointed because…

_____

_____

_____

_____

_____

_____

_____

_____

_____

_____

_____

_____

_____

_____

_____

_____

Writing Prompt

Can you believe...

_____

_____

_____

_____

_____

_____

_____

_____

_____

_____

_____

_____

_____

_____

Inspiration:

If you will change your thinking, God can change your life. In the following space, write out some of the ways God has been good to you.

_____

_____

_____

_____

_____

_____

_____

_____

_____

_____

_____

_____

_____

_____

_____

_____

WHAT THE SCRIPTURES SAY:

For if anyone is a hearer of the word and not a doer, he is like a man observing his natural face in a mirror; for he observes himself, goes away, and immediately forgets what kind of man he was. But he who looks into the perfect law of liberty and continues *in it,* and is not a forgetful hearer but a doer of the work, this one will be blessed in what he does.

James1: 23-25

As in water face reflects face, so a man's heart reveals the man.

Proverbs 27:19

A PRAYER FOR TODAY:

Heavenly Father, I pray that everything that I say and do will bring glory and honor to your name.

_____

_____

_____

_____

_____

_____

TAKEAWAY TRUTH: Everyone we meet is a mirror, reflecting our beliefs and perceptions back to us.

Principle 6

Bloom Where You're Planted

Preparation accelerates the promise

TRANSFORMING TRUTH:

Don't worry about things you cannot change. Keep a great attitude and keep blossoming right where you are. Make a decision to stay faithful and content at the place where God planted you. At the right time God will change those circumstances.

PONDER THIS: You can choose to be happy right where you are. Are you bearing good fruit? Are you being a great example? Make a decision to bloom where you're planted.

Writing Prompt

When will it be my time...

_____

_____

_____

_____

_____

_____

_____

_____

_____

_____

_____

_____

_____

_____

Writing Prompt

I'm anxious because...

_____

_____

_____

_____

_____

_____

_____

_____

_____

_____

_____

_____

_____

_____

_____

Writing Prompt

I'll be happy when I get married…

_____

_____

_____

_____

_____

_____

_____

_____

_____

_____

_____

_____

_____

_____

_____

Inspiration:

We find out what we are truly made of during the tough times of life. When we step out by faith, it activates the power of God. List below any challenges you are facing right now that are causing you to stretch and grow.

_____

_____

_____

_____

_____

_____

_____

_____

_____

_____

_____

_____

_____

_____

_____

WHAT THE SCRIPTURES SAY:

Let each one remain in the same calling in which he was called.

1 Corinthians 7:20

I am the vine, you are the branches. He who abides in Me, and I in him, bears much fruit; for without Me you can do nothing.

John 15:5

A PRAYER FOR TODAY:

Heavenly Father, please help me to be content in whatever season that I am in. I am only placing my trust and confidence in you.

_____

_____

_____

_____

_____

_____

_____

TAKEAWAY TRUTH: If you are not happy where you are, you will never get to where you want to be. I encourage you to trust God's perfect timing.

STEP THREE:

PREPARATION TIME IS NEVER WASTED TIME

Principle 7

Expand Your Awareness

*The more you continue to pursue personal growth
is the more you will have to offer.*

TRANSFORMING TRUTH:

If you consciously decide to expand your capacity, you will most definitely become a different person. You will look back and see how much you've grown.

PONDER THIS: Exposure is one of the first steps to a turnaround. Focus on becoming a better you and as you change, everything around you will change too.

Writing Prompt

What surprised you the most about your life or life in general?

_____

_____

_____

_____

_____

_____

_____

_____

_____

_____

_____

_____

_____

_____

_____

Writing Prompt

What does unconditional love look like for you?

_____

_____

_____

_____

_____

_____

_____

_____

_____

_____

_____

_____

_____

_____

_____

Writing Prompt

Write about your first love whether a person, place, or thing.

_____

_____

_____

_____

_____

_____

_____

_____

_____

_____

_____

_____

_____

_____

_____

_____

Inspiration

In the space below, make a list of the people in your life who genuinely support you, and who you can genuinely trust. (Then make time to hang out with them.)

WHAT THE SCRIPTURES SAY:

Enlarge the place of your tent, and then stretch out the curtains of your dwellings; Do not spare; lengthen your cords, and strengthen your stakes. For you shall expand to the right and to the left, and your descendants will inherit the nations, and make the desolate cities inhabited.

Isaiah 54: 2-3

May the Lord God of your fathers make you a thousand times more numerous than you are, and bless you as He has promised you!

Deuteronomy 1:11

A PRAYER FOR TODAY:

Heavenly Father, I ask that you expand my personal vision and purpose. Help me see myself, the way that you see me.

_____

_____

_____

_____

_____

_____

TAKEAWAY TRUTH: Surround yourself with people that are from different cultures, so you can cross pollinate and share great ideas.

Principle 8

Rewrite Your Story

If you want the present to be different from the past, study the past.

TRANSFORMING TRUTH:

In order for God to rewrite our story, we must willingly embrace a life of change.

PONDER THIS: God is the author of our story, and therefore He is the one who can beautifully rewrite it.

Writing Prompt

Dear Past me…

_____

_____

_____

_____

_____

_____

_____

_____

_____

_____

_____

_____

_____

_____

_____

Writing Prompt

Dear Future me…

_____

_____

_____

_____

_____

_____

_____

_____

_____

_____

_____

_____

_____

_____

_____

_____

Writing Prompt

How would you like to make this world a better place? How can you best share your gifts with the world?

_____

_____

_____

_____

_____

_____

_____

_____

_____

_____

_____

_____

_____

_____

_____

_____

Inspiration:

Where do you see yourself in the next five years?

_____

_____

_____

_____

_____

_____

_____

_____

_____

_____

_____

_____

_____

_____

_____

_____

WHAT THE SCRIPTURES SAY:

Therefore we also, since we are surrounded by so great a cloud of witnesses, let us lay aside every weight, and the sin which so easily ensnares *us,* and let us run with endurance the race that is set before us, looking unto Jesus, the author and finisher of *our* faith, who for the joy that was set before Him endured the cross, despising the shame, and has sat down at the right hand of the throne of God.

Hebrews 12: 1-2

A PRAYER FOR TODAY:

Heavenly Father, I know that nothing is wasted. Help me to search for how my past can add value to my present.

_____

_____

_____

_____

_____

_____

_____

_____

_____

Principle 9

Protect Your Progress

Preparation time is never wasted time

TRANSFORMING TRUTH:

Always prepare before you're ready. Your ability to make progress in life is directly related to your willingness to take responsibility for your actions.

PONDER THIS: Creating momentum in your life is everything, just like in business; it takes increasing the things that move you forward and decreasing those that hold you back.

Writing Prompt

What made you lose track of your time today?

_____

_____

_____

_____

_____

_____

_____

_____

_____

_____

_____

_____

_____

_____

_____

_____

Writing Prompt

List five things that you wish you invented.

_____

_____

_____

_____

_____

_____

_____

_____

_____

_____

_____

_____

_____

_____

_____

_____

_____

Writing Prompt

How did you spend your free time today?

_____

_____

_____

_____

_____

_____

_____

_____

_____

_____

_____

_____

_____

_____

_____

Inspiration:

In the space below, list three things that you do well.

_____

_____

_____

_____

_____

_____

_____

_____

_____

_____

_____

_____

_____

_____

_____

_____

_____

_____

WHAT THE SCRIPTURES SAY:

Do you not know that those who run in a race all run, but one receives the prize? Run in such a way that you may obtain *it*. [25] And everyone who competes *for the prize* is temperate in all things. Now they *do it* to obtain a perishable crown, but we *for* an imperishable *crown.* [26] Therefore I run thus: not with uncertainty. Thus I fight: not as *one who* beats the air. [27] But I discipline my body and bring *it* into subjection, lest, when I have preached to others, I myself should become disqualified.

1 Corinthians 9:24-27

The righteous shall flourish like a palm tree, he shall grow like a cedar in Lebanon.

Psalm 92:12

A PRAYER FOR TODAY:

Heavenly Father, please help me to stay focus on this journey. Help me not to look to the right or the left, but to look to the hills from whence comes my help.

_____

_____

_____

_____

STEP FOUR:

FAITH IT

Principle 10

If You Want to Be Successful, Be Less Accessible

Small minds are concerned with the ordinary,
great minds embraced the extraordinary.

TRANSFORMING TRUTH:

Being busy does not mean you are necessarily being productive.

PONDER THIS: Every time you say "yes" to something, you're saying "no" to something else. You can't do it all if you want to do anything well.

Writing Prompt

Write down three "bigger than life" dreams, goals, or plans for your life. Then write three specific actions you can take today to help make those dreams become realities:

_____

_____

_____

_____

_____

_____

_____

_____

_____

_____

_____

_____

_____

Writing Prompt:

Describe some areas in which you would like to see some real changes in your life. How will you begin?

_____

_____

_____

_____

_____

_____

_____

_____

_____

_____

_____

_____

_____

Writing Prompt:

What are your daily routines?

_____

_____

_____

_____

_____

_____

_____

_____

_____

_____

_____

_____

_____

_____

_____

_____

Inspiration:

Start paying attention to incredible opportunities. In the following space, reflect on the words above and then describe examples of being less accessible so that progress can be possible.

_____

_____

_____

_____

_____

_____

_____

_____

_____

_____

_____

_____

_____

_____

WHAT THE SCRIPTURES SAY:

Delight yourself also in the LORD, and He shall give you the desires of your heart.

Psalm 37:4

Commit your works to the LORD, and your thoughts will be established.

Proverbs 16:3

A PRAYER FOR TODAY:

Thank you Lord, you are able to do exceeding abundantly above all that we ask or think, according to your power that work in us.

_____

_____

_____

_____

_____

_____

_____

_____

TAKEAWAY TRUTH: Success is an inside job. All of life gets better when we get better.

Principle 11

Survey Your Circle

Live confidently, speak confidently, and walk confidently in the direction of your dreams.

TRANSFORMING TRUTH:

The old adage sums this up perfectly "A man is known by the company he keeps."

PONDER THIS: Building great friendships is everything. Our friends play a major influence on how we think, feel, and behave. Make sure you survey your circle frequently.

Writing Prompt

What qualities do you look for in your friends?

_____

_____

_____

_____

_____

_____

_____

_____

_____

_____

_____

_____

_____

_____

Writing Prompt

Do you enjoy meeting new people? Why or Why not?

_____

_____

_____

_____

_____

_____

_____

_____

_____

_____

_____

_____

_____

_____

_____

_____

Writing Prompt

Do you consider yourself a good friend? Why or Why not?

_____

_____

_____

_____

_____

_____

_____

_____

_____

_____

_____

_____

_____

_____

Inspiration:

Learn how to diversify your inputs, influences, and experiences. In the space below, write how you can better diversify yourself.

_____

_____

_____

_____

_____

_____

_____

_____

_____

_____

_____

_____

_____

_____

_____

_____

WHAT THE SCRIPTURES SAY:

Do not be deceived: "Evil company corrupts good habits."

1 Corinthians 15: 33

He who walks with wise men will be wise, But the companion of fools will be destroyed.

Proverbs 13: 20

A PRAYER FOR TODAY: Lord, today I ask for wisdom in choosing my friends. Help me not only to choose for today, but to choose my friends for tomorrow.

TAKEAWAY TRUTH:

Choose friends that stretch, motivate, and encourage you. Your friends will have a major influence on your life.

_____

_____

_____

_____

_____

_____

_____

_____

Principle 12

Master Your Moves

Separation is a Requirement for Elevation

TRANSFORMING TRUTH:

In this season, refuse to be an average jack of all trades and become a master of one.

PONDER THIS: Be engaged with your work. Do what's never been done. Try what's never been tried. Make it all your own.

Writing Prompt

In the following space, list 10 things you must start doing to be successful.

_____

_____

_____

_____

_____

_____

_____

_____

_____

_____

_____

_____

_____

_____

_____

Writing Prompt

In the space below, list 10 things you must start doing to be happy.

_____

_____

_____

_____

_____

_____

_____

_____

_____

_____

_____

_____

_____

_____

_____

Writing Prompt

What actions can you take to meet your personal goals?

_____

_____

_____

_____

_____

_____

_____

_____

_____

_____

_____

_____

_____

_____

_____

Inspiration

In the space below, list all your gifts.

_____

_____

_____

_____

_____

_____

_____

_____

_____

_____

_____

_____

_____

_____

_____

_____

_____

WHAT THE SCRIPTURES SAY:

Whoever has no rule over his own spirit, is like a city broken down, without walls.

Proverbs 25:28

The soul of a lazy man desires, and has nothing; but the soul of the diligent shall be made rich.

Proverbs 13:4

But you, be strong and do not let your hands be weak, for your work shall be rewarded!"

2 Chronicles 15:7

A PRAYER FOR TODAY:

Heavenly Father, please help me to further master my gifts and talents. Your word said that my gift will make room for me.

_____

_____

_____

_____

_____

_____

_____

TAKEAWAY TRUTH: Even our worst experiences in life are really blessings in disguise. Nothing is wasted.

FINAL THOUGHTS

I have been journaling on and off for the past five years and during tough times, it has been truly therapeutic. By committing to this writing process, you have a record of what has been happening in your life.

I want to encourage you to consciously set aside time for personal reflection and ask yourself the following questions: Am I living up to my core values and personal mission? Am I making a positive impact on the world?

In order to improve our chances of reaching our goals, self-awareness is critical. We have to be good to ourselves first, before we can be good to others. On that note, I leave you with this; it's never wise to pour from an empty cup.

Printed in the United States
By Bookmasters